The Micro-Niche Method™

The pathway to premium pricing and increased profitability for today's CPAs

David Wolfskehl

Dedicated to my Mom, Dad,
Puppy, Buddy and Marcie

Contents

Introduction

Introduction

As a CPA, you know about numbers. You take pride in delivering measurable results for your clients. Your work is quantifiable and performed according to time-tested methods.

But how about *your* numbers? Are your quarterly revenues what they could be? Are you maximizing your billable hours? Are you selling your services at the highest possible rate? Do you scramble for new business, or does new business come to you?

In today's business environment, you can't just sit back and run your business the way you did five or ten years ago. You need to stay sharp and adapt to new challenges. You need to be proactive. You need effective strategies for positioning yourself in the marketplace.

It has become axiomatic in business that for long-term growth and success, you need to be number one in your market. Maybe – like Avis – you can be number two. But never number three. Why? Because the best clients want the number one provider. They will pay a premium for expert service. They will not seek out the firm that is trailing in the pack.

But you say, "Deloitte is number one! They have revenues of $26 billion a year and employ 170,000 people! How can we possibly dream of being number one?"

True – you may not be number one in the global CPA market. And you may not be number one in your regional marketing niche.

But you can absolutely be number one in your *micro-niche. The Micro-niche method*™ will show you how. And being number one in your micro-niche will translate into a better bottom line.

What's a micro-niche? It's your self-defined segment of the marketplace. The specialized area where you excel. The tightly focused niche where you rule.

But you say, "If we narrow our focus we will lose customers. We need to be broad. We need to be a jack-of-all trades."

The Micro-niche method™ is not about cutting services. It's about strengthening those services at which you or your individual partners excel. It reveals how developing your micro-niche will allow you to increase your fees and increase productivity. Clients will pay more for the industry leader who provides the exact service they need. They can't afford not to!

Let's face it – within the CPA industry there is tremendous uniformity of services. Your firm has probably built one or more niches within your profession, and chances are very good that many of your competitors have chosen the same niches. Whenever I look at the websites of CPA firms, I see the same niches regardless of the size of the firm. Developing your micro-niche differentiates you from all other local or regional firms and removes you from direct competition. Imagine truly eliminating most of your competition! Is that an exciting thought for you? *The Micro-niche method*™ will show you how to do it.

Call it what you will – specializing in a specific area, or capitalizing on your expertise, or building a micro-niche – this is a business growth strategy that emphasizes a particular sub-category within what you already do. Because your micro-niche is built upon your existing strength – one you are already doing – it significantly increases the chance for success.

Your domination of your micro-niche allows you to do four things:

1. Charge premium prices for these very special services.

2. Eliminate other firms from competition because they do not and often cannot compete with the very specialized services you offer or the way you are able to deliver those services.

3. Increase the efficiency with which you produce the work.

4. Leverage the power of your effective marketing.

Within a larger firm, micro-niches can be very profitable because the professional with a micro-niche quickly comes to know the target customer group so well it is possible to meet their needs better than other firms – including those firms that are occasionally selling services to this micro-niche. This customer knowledge or customer intimacy is one added value that justifies charging higher prices.

Within a smaller firm your micro-niche will allow you to charge large firm fees and make you the safe choice.

The Micro-niche method™: Your competitors are doing it. And now you can do it too.

David Wolfskehl

1

What is a
Micro-Niche?

• 1 •

What Is a Micro-Niche?

The Business Dictionary at www.allbusiness.com defines "micro-niche" as "the particular specialty in which a firm or person finds they prosper. Micro-niche strategy in marketing is to market to a small but lucrative portion of the market. The small size of the micro-niche generally ensures efficient marketing efforts and few if any direct competitors."

Let's expand on this definition in a few ways:

- A micro-niche is a sub-category within the practice area.

- A micro-niche is an area in which you have significant experience and knowledge (or in which you can acquire knowledge).

- A micro-niche meets the particular needs of a defined group of potential clients.

- A micro-niche is characterized by special knowledge and experience for which clients will pay a premium price.

Specializing is a familiar practice for many professionals. A physician might specialize in orthopedics, an attorney might specialize in estate law, an accountant might specialize in mergers and acquisitions, and an actuary might specialize in life insurance. Their fees reflect the value of their specializations.

Of course, many CPAs specialize. But if you look at the books of business or at the websites and marketing materials of most CPA firms, you will probably find a ninety-percent match in the services and/or products offered by each accounting firm. The areas of specialty are essentially the same across all accountants in any region. When this happens, there are no niches – *in the marketplace, the firms are indistinguishable.* The client can't tell one from another. So what does the client do? They select the firm with the lowest price. Or the one physically close to their home or office.

And your firm or partnership is forced to compete on the basis of price.

Your Value Proposition

When you define and market a specialty area, you re-define your value proposition. You differentiate your firm by the micro-niche and you can then re-define the primary value proposition for all clients. Because the services offered to micro-niche clients are specialized and require a higher level of expertise (one you probably already have, but have not defined and figured out how to market), these services will need a unique value proposition.

For your clients, this is an important difference. You offer a choice they have rarely been given in the past.

You might state your value proposition in terms of the value of the level of specialization you offer. Your premium pricing for your micro-niche services will be higher than your standard fee structure. You might also state your value proposition in terms of your uniquely branded credentials to offer a uniquely defined and specialized service package.

Clients Respond to Micro-Niche Providers

When your firm stands out in your self-defined micro-niche, customers respond. You can see this principle at work every day.

Let's say you own a BMW. Down the street is a generic garage that services all makes and models of cars. Ten minutes farther away is a garage that specializes in BMWs. You might take your car to the generic garage for an oil change. But if there were real work involved, wouldn't you gladly pay extra to entrust your valuable BMW to a specialist? Of course you would.

Does the idea of growing your practice by narrowing your focus seem counterintuitive? It's not. Building a micro-niche allows you to differentiate yourself from the hundreds of other CPAs in your market. Clients will seek you out and pay a premium for your specialized services.

If you had a sore back, would go to your family physician – or would you travel an extra half-hour to visit a back specialist?

If you needed tax advice on your offshore investments, would you go to a local storefront CPA or to a professional who specialized in protecting offshore assets?

In everyday life, we routinely seek the highest level of specialized assistance. When seeking service that can make a difference to their lives or to their bottom line, clients will seek out a micro-niche provider and:

- Reject providers who are less qualified.

- Pay more for the micro-niche service.

- Travel further to get the micro-niche service.

- Wait longer for the micro-niche service.

A Niche and a Micro-Niche

Niches can be big. Micro-niches are subsets of niches and are tightly focused. The way you define and build your new micro-niche might mean specializing in some singular aspect of one of the niches served by everyone in your field. By becoming an expert in a micro-niche, you differentiate yourself more clearly and you create the capacity to charge premium pricing. For example, a physician might specialize in orthopedic medicine. This would be a niche. Yet, the physician might go even further and specialize in the care and treatment of hands, or perhaps just fingers. This would be a micro-niche.

Similarly, for an accounting firm, specializing in international tax issues is a niche. A *micro-niche* might be built by a practitioner who has work experience in India and in the U.S., and who truly knows how business works and how companies pay taxes in both countries. This practitioner can talk to the CEO of a company doing business in both countries and know that when she tells the CEO she understands a particular issue, she really understands the issue and the CEO knows she understands. She will have credibility with the potential client. She will be much more current with changes in the laws (and their interpretation) in both countries because it is easier to keep up with one market than with the whole world.

Another micro-niche within international tax issues might be a specialization in Chinese and U.S. tax issues. Or Brazilian-U.S. tax issues. Just within this niche, the possibilities for micro-niches are numerous.

As the needs of potential clients continue to become more complex, people will continue to gravitate toward specialists or experts. They will seek out those CPAs who have the knowledge and experience to meet their particular needs in a way a generalist cannot. Because micro-niches focus on a specialized area in which you have expertise, you are in a unique position to win their attention and their business.

See the Client's Point of View

An important consideration when building and defining a micro-niche is to define your micro-niche from the point of view of the client's need. Many CPA firms tend to think of their work only in terms of the deliverable. You know you have a great product (the deliverable). But before they hire you, clients and prospective clients have no way of knowing your product is superior. Many professionals believe there is little opportunity to differentiate their firm based on the product because other professionals presumably deliver the same great product or the client does not have the in-depth knowledge needed to know the difference between the deliverables. Many CPA clients are not sophisticated enough in the area of your expertise to know the difference between the deliverables of various firms. It is up to you to use both the difference in the deliverables and the micro-niche specialization to persuade them of the superiority of your value proposition.

Identify Pain Points

One of the most exciting ways to define a micro-niche business or to identify new ways to differentiate your firm from the competition is by identifying a client/customer pain point in your marketplace and developing a unique value proposition that eliminates or alleviates that pain.

Removing risk and pain from any business transaction opens doors for new business success. Businesses have been doing this for centuries. When you can identify a product the public wants and the pain that is associated with the purchase of that product, you can create an uncontested business space by offering that product without the pain.

The Difference Is Marketing

What CPA firms need to understand is that it is much easier to differentiate yourself in terms of the way the great product is delivered or by speaking in terms of the problems you solve or the client pain you eliminate with your specialized service. Building a micro-niche and explaining the services you offer based on the unique background you have to deliver a better product and deliver it in a better way is the best way to differentiate your firm from all of the other similar firms in town. You need to *market* your micro-niche.

Blockbuster, Netflix, and Redbox

The movie rental business provides a good example of how a small company can find a micro-niche in the marketplace, exploit it, and take over market share from established competitors.

Back in 1977, the only ways that Hollywood movie studios could deliver their products to the consumer was in movie theatres and on network television. These were the markets for feature films. In that same year, the Japanese electronics company JVC introduced the first consumer videocassettes in the VHS format. Within a few years, a new market was born: feature films on VHS that you could take home and watch on your own VCR. For the first time, you didn't have to go to a movie theatre to watch an uncut, first-run movie.

For Hollywood, the home rental business was a new revenue stream. Soon there were video stores offering videotapes for sale, and the equipment to play them at home. A niche business had been created.

But people always want more value for less money. Sure enough, the home video niche market soon developed symptoms of customer pain. Did customers want to build video libraries? Was every movie worth its purchase price for a single viewing? Was there any reason to *own* a copy of a movie? The solution to client pain was the creation of yet another niche: the rise of the video *rental* store. These stores did less selling of videos and more renting. Eventually they stopped selling the equipment and left that part of the business to electronics stores. For additional revenue, they began selling candy and popcorn in movie theater packaging. As new and better formats and equipment came to market, the stores adapted.

Over time, **Blockbuster** bought out or eclipsed the smaller stores and emerged as the video rental industry leader. Their business model seemed indestructible: customers rented videos (and later on, DVDs), watched them at home, and then returned them. By 2010, Blockbuster grew to over 5,000 store locations in the U.S. and seventeen foreign countries, with over $4 billion in revenues.

Then customers began to focus on the new pain of the retail cost, often $4.00 for a single night. Blockbuster also charged notoriously high late fees – another source of pain. And, you had to drive to the video store and choose a movie from those that were available at the moment. On Saturday night, the first-run release that you wanted was never in stock.

NetFlix responded to this customer pain by creating a micro-niche. First, they introduced an unlimited subscription model. Then they eliminated late fees altogether. They also eliminated the need to go pick up your movies because they arrived in your mailbox or were streamed online. By 2007, NetFlix had taken a big bite of the home movie market and is now posting revenues of $1.6 billion a year.

Yet in this competitive market there was room for *another* micro-niche. What was it? Anyone who has ever worked retail understands that we love impulse buys. We see something that we like and we snap it up. To meet this need a new micro-niche was created by **Redbox**. These small red kiosks are appearing everywhere – outside drug stores, inside supermarkets – offering a limited selection of the most popular movies for a $1.00 rental fee and no late fees.

In 2007, Redbox, a subsidiary of Coinstar, had three percent of the market. By 2009 they had 22,000 of their kiosks throughout the U.S. By late 2010, they controlled thirty percent of the market and posted 2009 revenues of $733 million – a 99.1 percent increase over 2008!

Blockbuster gave up on its original business model, filed for bankruptcy protection and is now advertising a deal allowing them to rent movies to the public thirty days earlier than their competition. They are also charging no late fees, offering movies online at the same low price as other rentals, and they have started placing rental kiosks (just like Redbox) near other popular retail stores. Many people think this is too little too late – Blockbuster has gone from being an innovator to an 800-pound gorilla to a company that is copying the competition. It's showing all the classic signs of being on the slow spiral of death.

By remaining focused on client pain, these start-up companies were able to develop solutions that alleviated the pain for their clients. Maintaining a focus on client pain and ways to alleviate every pain enabled these companies to slay the 800-pound gorilla in their marketplace.

2

Why You Should Build a Micro-Niche

Why You Should Build a Micro-Niche

There are compelling reasons why you should build a micro-niche for your firm.

Premium Pricing

If you are perceived as an expert, you can charge premium prices. People who are considered experts in virtually every field and in every line of work earn higher salaries or fees because of their expertise. When people think of you as an expert, they assume that you have some special knowledge or skill and that you have the inside scoop on an industry. When you are perceived and paid as an expert you earn more money from less work.

Depending on the type of services you provide to clients, the type of firm you are in, and your location, you can expect to charge a premium on work you do in your micro-niche. As an expert – who provides an excellent product appropriately packaged and delivered well – your clients will expect to pay a premium rate for your work.

In today's world of specialization, people feel a need for an expert more and more often. They tell themselves that their need is unique and warrants focus and specialization. Because their need is important, it is served by experts and specialists who have:

- More extensive training.

- More focused experience.

- More knowledge.

This uniqueness factor builds the expectation and the assumption that the expert can deliver a product of higher value, a greater benefit, and a more valuable service than competitors. This creates the expectation of paying premium pricing.

Attraction

If you are perceived as an expert, business will come to you. When new clients come to you with little or no effort on your part, you will reduce the amount of time and money you need to invest in other sales and marketing strategies to build your practice. When you are perceived as an expert the word gets around quickly in the industry. You will also have new opportunities available to have your expertise touted by others (see the marketing section). You will still need to go out and bring in new clients, and you will still need to market your firm, but people will also search you out to solve their important needs also.

WHY BUILD A MICRO-NICHE?

o **Premium Pricing – Clients will travel further, wait longer, and pay a premium price for an expert who can solve their high-risk problems.**

o **Attraction – Business comes to experts, not generic providers.**

o **Branding – Marketing your firm is easier because you are a recognized expert in your field.**

We live in a time when people value expertise. We believe we should seek out specialists and experts to meet our needs. We have been trained by the medical and legal professions to seek out experts and specialists because they are better trained, more experienced, and better able to meet our needs.

Not only will business come to you because you are an expert, but if you build upon the importance of the customer's needs, clients will be coming to you from a greater distance or through more difficult circumstances, and this will become a customer claim that reinforces the value of your expertise and of the services you provide to clients.

When you provide outstanding service to clients and you consistently deliver on your value proposition, you can expect your satisfied clients to tell others about you and to make referrals to you. Clients will tell their business associates, co-workers, friends, family members and others that they obtain the specific service you offer from a specialist. We only look for experts when we believe we need assistance with a significant issue. When the issue is resolved to our satisfaction by the expert we choose, we tell others about the expert who saved our bacon.

Branding

When clients perceive you as an expert, you have a way to differentiate yourself in the market. You can build your brand power.

It is unlikely that your CPA firm is the only game in town. You are likely in direct competition with many other firms just like yours. When you build a micro-niche and become recognized as an expert you will be set apart from the competition. Differentiating yourself is a key marketing strategy (see below). Standing head and shoulders above the crowd (because of your expert status) makes it much easier for people to see you and turn to you.

A Micro-Niche: Corporations Going Green

For example, if your CPA firm specializes in corporate tax and accounting, but you focus on large corporations, you have probably distinguished yourself from half of the other corporate accounting firms in the region. If two of your firm's partners have worked together to learn everything there is to learn about taxes, financing, tax credits, and the like about large corporations that decide to "go green" with their headquarters, manufacturing plants, or retail outlets (as Wal-Mart is doing), you have the basis of a micro-niche. When another large corporation decides to go green, your micro-niche will now distinguish your firm from all of the other firms in the region. Further, because of the vast knowledge acquired by your two partners in order to serve the needs of their existing clients, you have the information you need to market that expertise effectively to other companies. Your two-pronged marketing approach (referrals from your satisfied clients and the knowledge of what information will make the sale to other companies) has great like-lihood of success.

3

From Commodity
to Expert

• 3 •

From Commodity to Expert

Every day, I hear CPA firms talk about fee pressure. I also hear them talk about the frustration and the time spent preparing and answering a large number of RFPs. This is the price of being a commodity. CPAs tell me their clients do not deal with them in ways that make them feel respected as professionals. They believe they are constantly hassled about price and that the risk of their clients leaving for another firm is constantly hanging over them. They also commonly tell me they do not feel their marketing is effective.

My response to these complaints can only be, "Stop being a commodity!" The only way to move your firm from commodity status is to become an expert with a well-defined micro-niche. This will allow you to target your marketing and get more clients by focusing on the right prospects. You must recognize that no firm can or should be an expert in everything.

If you want to stop being a commodity and command the respect you deserve, you must:

- Analyze your client base for areas in which you excel.

- Analyze your competition for areas in which you can stand apart.

- Analyze your team for unrecognized areas of experience or expertise.

- Invest in cultivating needed expertise within your staff.

- Think smaller in order to grow larger.

- Focus your marketing.

- Sharpen your focus on targeted prospects.

4

What is a
Micro-Niche?

• 4 •

Defining Your Micro-Niche

Identifying four or five people for whom you provide the same service is a very good start toward defining a micro-niche. But it is only a beginning. Building a micro-niche involves more than deciding that you are serving a micro-niche. It also involves more than just having four or five clients in a particular industry or who depend on you for a specific service. Defining a micro-niche also requires specialized knowledge both needed and valued by prospective clients.

Steps to Defining Your Micro-Niche

1. Research. You need to do some careful research and analysis and be sure that you know what steps must be taken before you can credibly claim expertise and expand your presence in the specific industry. You also need to research and analyze how much growth potential the micro-niche offers for your business, and for how long. You can only decide how to maximize your opportunities when you have answered these questions.

2. Characterize your expertise. How will you use your knowledge, skill or experience to differentiate yourself from your competitors? It is not

enough to define or characterize your expertise in "insider jargon." Instead, you must take the next step and draw the connecting lines between your expertise and the specific client needs or pain points that expertise enables you to alleviate. You must define your expertise and the services you offer from the client's point of view.

Your ability to define your area of expertise and the value of the services you offer will define the limits within which you will try to market your micro-niche business. Until you can create a client-need-focused definition of the service, you will not be able to convince prospective clients that you offer something different, better or greater.

3. Listen to your clients. The way to identify and understand client pain is to listen to your clients and to prospective clients. There should be a conversation with every client that does business with your firm about changes in the industry, about changes in the client's needs, about decisions the client is trying to make, and about strategic changes in the direction of the client's company.

   Those conversations should help you to identify common areas of change, need or pain. When you determine that your firm has the capabilities to alleviate that pain, meet the need or assist with the change, it is time to have deeper conversations with the appropriate clients or prospects. In these conversations, the goal will be to understand the causes of the pain, related needs, pains or changes and the effects of those pains on the client's business or life. Until you understand the client's pain on a profound level you will not be able to shape a service that answers the need.

4. Don't forget the human element. There is something to be said for an approach to determining the micro-niche by simply choosing an area to focus on because you are interested in that industry or because you enjoy a particular type of work best. This process not only allows you professional success but also provides personal fulfillment.

Questions to Ask Yourself

Defining a new micro-niche for your firm cannot happen on the field of dreams. There is absolutely no reason to believe that if you build it, they will come. Instead, your micro-niche must be defined in response to clear and sufficient client pain or need. Here are the key questions you should ask regarding any micro-niche brought to the table:

- Does it address the needs of a cluster of current clients?

- What industries are they in? Do we know enough about each?

- What other commonalities do they have?

- Are they served by individual members of our firm, or does everyone in the firm have some special focus on clients in a specific industry?

- Is there enough opportunity now to justify the cost and effort to build a micro-niche?

- Is the need likely to extend far enough into the future to be worthwhile?

You might (and usually do) discover that your firm actually has more than one significant cluster of clients in different industries or with specific service needs. They might be served by different members of your staff. Then you must decide whether you have the time and the resources to try to build a presence in more than one micro-niche. You might create a strategy to develop one micro-niche at a time over a period of years. Often, each partner develops a micro-niche or each niche develops multiple micro niches with these niches.

Unmatched Service and Expertise

When you deal with the same issues and problems on a regular basis, you and your team typically become very efficient about producing the work and very knowledgeable about the needs of your clients. Any firm that focuses time and attention on particular activities repetitively will develop processes and procedures to save time, reduce duplicated effort, and reduce the margin for error. This increases customer satisfaction – they get their work faster and with fewer errors – and profitability for the firm.

The world tells you what you're good at. The experiences in your life will give you the specific knowledge for building your micro-niche. If you have an established firm, the best way to decide where to build a micro-niche might be to look at your book of business and see where there is a large cluster of clients. Then you can carve out your micro-niche by building upon what the world has already recognized in you.

A focus on the same kind of clients with the same needs and issues enables you to gain the intimate knowledge of their business that remains closed to others. Not only do you become more knowledgeable of your micro-niche from and through your clients, you are also the first to know about other evolving or emerging needs of those clients. This positions your firm in the driver's seat to create another micro-niche business to meet those needs as well.

Building your micro-niche, then, positions your firm within the marketplace as the specialists offering clients with specific and important needs the unique knowledge and services they need.

You are able to charge premium prices for services within that micro-niche as you solve important issues for your clients.

You will increase the efficiency of your firm as you complete similar work on a regular basis.

You will also achieve more focused marketing and increased profitability.

5

How to Build
Your Micro-Niche

• 5 •

How to Build Your Micro-Niche

The first element of your micro-niche is the foundation. You will need to invest the time to thoroughly research the opportunity offered by the micro-niche and evaluate your firm's ability to dominate that micro-niche. Here are the eight key steps in building a micro-niche:

1. Identify the size of the micro-niche. How big is the industry? How much is it growing or declining? Is your city becoming a hub for this industry, or are companies leaving town to relocate in the industry hub? What practice development opportunities are available to you? How will you maximize those opportunities?

2. Maximize your relationships with trade groups for speaking and consulting opportunities. These opportunities put you in the presence of potential clients. Sharing your expertise might be the way to show them you know how to end their pain.

3. Identify the pains clients feel and figure out how to offer the service they need in a way that eliminates or alleviates their pain.

4. Identify how much of the micro-niche you can hope to own. How many businesses in the chosen micro-niche are located near you? How many of those businesses can you hope to bring into your firm? Can you do business with others that are located

outside your city? How many can you reasonably expect to make your clients? In other words, how much can you maximize the opportunity to grow your practice by following this path?

5. Conduct a SWOT analysis of the competition: their Strengths, Weaknesses, Opportunities, and Threats. How many competitors are there in your city? How many potential local clients are being served by a competitor in another city? What are the strengths, weaknesses and opportunities of each of your competitors? How does your firm compare to the competition? How can you different-iate your firm over and against your competitors? What competitor weaknesses can you capitalize on to grow your place in the micro-niche? What marketing strategies will be necessary to do so?

6. Plan your messaging and your marketing. It is important to start with the message. Clarify what you want to say before you start down the road of how to get the message out. To some degree, the message determines the medium. How will you differentiate your firm and your expertise over and against your competitors? How do prospective clients in this micro-niche want to hear your message? What marketing strategies will enable you to reach them with the right message in the right medium in the right place at the right time? How will you spread the word?

7. Understand the needs of those clients. What can you do to offer them additional value? How can you meet the specific needs of

these clients consistently with flawless execution? What emerging needs can you identify and meet? How can your experience and expertise deliver greater value to the client?

8. Grow your micro-niche. Get busy, get out there, and get the clients. If you accomplish each of the first five steps, you will have everything you need to build your micro-niche and grow your practice. Practice development for a CPA firm is not rocket science. It does require thought, planning, process development, and commitment to success.

   Remember that your firm is unique. There is no one-size-fits-all micro-niche solution. The key is to transition your program from the conference room to the real world. You'll quickly learn insights and develop strategies based on your experience and client feedback. In other words, *just do it!*

   By discovering for yourself how you can/do serve a micro-niche, considering what you hope to accomplish, and following the eight basic steps to building a micro-niche, you will be well on your way to growing your business and to growing it in a profitable direction – in a way that makes you so much more than a commodity. Practice development is like anything else in life – if you do your homework, focus your attention in the right ways, and step out knowledgeably, you can earn your right to claim expertise in a particular industry or segment.

Continuous Evaluation

D evelopment of processes and checklists is important when developing a micro-niche. It will be important to learn from each micro-niche-building experience lessons to make the next effort easier and faster because building the structure, the mindset and the processes for continuous micro-niche development will carry your firm successfully and profitably into the future.

There are no simple guidelines regarding the frequency with which a firm should build a new micro-niche. The external variables (changes in client need and pain, the economy, etc.) and internal variables (the bandwidth of the firm to manage ongoing work and the intensive work of building and marketing a new boutique business) will dictate the firm's capabilities.

Building a micro-niche is not without risk for a firm. Micro-niches can shrink over time and other firms can decide to compete with you for a share of the market. This risk underlies and underscores the emphasis upon evaluating the potential size of the micro-niche from the outset.

A firm would also do well periodically to re-evaluate the strength of the market. Further, the risk also argues for the creation of multiple micro-niches within a single firm. In fact, it is very likely that most firms have the foundation for at least two or three micro-niches by the time they start thinking about using micro-niche building to achieve practice growth.

• •

Quick Case Study

Here is an example of how a micro-niche might be developed. You are the managing partner in a mid-sized accounting firm who wants to grow your book of business. You look at your litigation support group and notice that you work with a number of lawyers who send you work from clients who have overseas real estate. Although initially this was very difficult for your firm to work with, over time it has become a practice area in which your firm has expertise. You know that your competitors rarely have opportunities to work with these special issues, and because they do it only occasionally, it is very difficult for them to be effective.

Your expertise allows you to:

- Keep on top of trends.

- Know the hidden issues that crop up.

- Have access to other professionals who can help support you.

- Provide your clients with a better level of service than your competitors.

Do you think you can own this micro-niche? We think you can.

6

Going from a Micro-Niche to a Boutique

• 6 •

Going from a Micro-Niche to a Boutique

Webster's Dictionary defines "boutique" as *"1. A small fashionable shop, b. a small shop within a large department store; 2. A small company that offers highly specialized services or products."*

- Your micro-niche is your specialized expertise. But it does not exist in a vacuum. Therefore,

- The boutique is the total experience created when the client accesses your micro-niche expertise.

The boutique focuses singularly on a specific and narrowly defined group of clients (and prospective clients) about whom they know a great deal. The boutique also focuses on offering the particular expertise-driven products and/or services needed or desired by the client base.

The Client Experience

Consider Starbucks and McDonalds for a moment. Both sell and serve coffee. Starbucks builds its premium brand not just on the coffee but on the customer experience – the stores, the aromas, the service, the furnishings, the free wi-fi connections.

McDonald's advertises "premium roast coffee" made with "100% Arabica beans." They advertise that in every McDonald's restaurant, the pot of coffee is made fresh every thirty minutes.

A cup of basic black coffee at McDonald's costs $1.35. At Starbucks it's $1.55. Twenty cents more – but more significantly, it's almost fifteen percent more. And Starbucks coffee prices go up from $1.55 to over $5.00 each for some "grande" drinks.

The fact that the Starbucks coffee product is perceived to be superior and carries a higher price tag is only the first step. Starbucks doesn't just sell their coffee in an ordinary fast-food environment. In every one of their over 17,000 stores around the world, they have created a boutique environment that provides an enhanced customer experience.

Starbucks is perceived to be the coffee expert, and this is what their business is built on. Many CPAs will read about a boutique business within an accounting firm and laugh it off as unnecessary overkill. That would be a mistake. Most people prefer to have special issues handled by experts. Most also expect to pay a premium price in order to avail themselves of the specialist's expertise. They also expect a different client experience.

Case Study:
Tax Preparation Services

Think about the different types of clients and their different expectations of the national tax preparation chains. They serve customers and clients at various levels.

1. **Basic level.** The customer walks in off the street, or the CPA firm makes the forms and the calculations available online at no charge. There is little or no profit. The only upside to this effort is that the firm hopes that young customers will develop brand loyalty, and that when they are making significant money they will still patronize the firm.

2. **Middle-income level.** This client is the one who needs some help and who has a few other forms. These people come to the office and meet with a preparer in a room where five or ten other meetings are occurring. These people might need a Schedule A or D. These people pay a set price per form. The client may choose to have the completed return filed electronically for a fee, and the completed return is delivered in a plain white envelope. These clients produce some profit.

3. **Executive.** These clients own businesses or they are self-employed or have several sources of income and investments. They meet with an executive preparer (more knowledge and experience) in a private office. They pay a base fee plus the cost

to prepare each form. The cost of electronic filing is included in the base fee. Their completed returns are delivered in special envelopes made of high-quality paper and embossed with the name of the company. The executive clients, in other words, have a different client experience from the average clients.

4. **High-net-worth.** These clients don't patronize national chains; they are more likely to have their taxes done at a boutique firm that caters to them. These are the top clients who demand specialized services and the highest level of personal service. The stakes can be very high; a poor accounting decision may cost millions of dollars or even send the client to prison. These clients are highly profitable for the CPA micro-niche boutique.

For example, in 1984, the IRS began looking into country singer Willie Nelson's tax returns going back to 1972. After an intensive investigation, the IRS declared that Nelson had underpaid taxes for six years. Nelson had taken invalid deductions after investing in tax shelters that the IRS had subsequently disqualified. In June 1990, a tax court ruled in favor of the government, and Nelson agreed to pay $6 million in back taxes, plus more than $10 million in penalties and interest. Fortunately, unlike actor Wesley Snipes, who was convicted of tax evasion and in December 2010 reported to federal prison, Nelson was allowed to work off his debt.

Who was Nelson's CPA? We don't know, but we do know that Nelson is making sure he gets expert, specialized tax advice. When the stakes are high, wealthy clients will pay a premium for the highest level of professional service. If they can't get it from you, they will get it from your competitor.

The Boutique Client Experience

There are many ways to create a unique and desirable client experience within a CPA firm. The experience is defined by how the client is treated when calling or visiting the firm's offices; by access to other specialized services or opportunities; or even by special access to your CPAs or to events sponsored by the firm for its best clients.

Here are a few examples of ways you can provide boutique clients with a special client experience:

- Boutique clients always work with the same people (from receptionist to accountant or partner). The people they talk with in the firm know them, their needs, the services they obtain from the firm, and are prepared to answer many questions immediately. If the person they need to speak with is not available when they call, they receive a call back within one hour from the person who was not available or from the receptionist with a direct answer to their questions.

- Boutique clients are never kept waiting. Their appointments are "cushioned" with an extra fifteen or thirty minutes between the expert's previous appointment and the boutique client's appointment. If, for some reason, the expert they is running late, they are notified and given a new time for the meeting and a reason for the delay. (Yes, we know that earlier we said that clients would be willing to wait longer to see a micro-niche expert. This is true – until you get to the very highest levels. These top clients will pay a premium for instant service.)

- Boutique clients receive additional communication (follow-up notes, holiday greetings, birthday/anniversary wishes).

- Appointments with boutique clients are held in a conference room or in a well-appointed office (not in the same small and cluttered office as every tax client), and these clients are always offered something to drink (coffee, tea, soda, water) during the meeting. When reasonable, meetings are scheduled near a mealtime and the client is invited to lunch or dinner after the meeting is concluded. This builds the relationship, provides opportunities for the CPA to learn more about the client and his/her business and creates opportunities to have the kind of conversations that frequently lead to referrals.

- Boutique clients often ask you to meet with them in their own offices. Meeting in the client's office is both convenient for the client and an opportunity for the CPA. Meetings held in the client's office are an opportunity to see the client in his or her work setting, to see how his or her business operates and to meet other executives.

- Boutique clients receive the highest level of personal service. Laws, tax codes, property valuations and government regulations change daily. While a written (or email) notification of changes might be sent to all clients of the firm, you might offer boutique clients an opportunity to speak with your expert (either face to face or by phone) about changes the business must make to comply, or how the tax change will affect cash flow and profitability.

You might invite micro-niche boutique clients to a dinner during an industry event or conference. You might invite a high-profile expert to make a presentation before or after the meal. Many businesses of all kinds give gifts to prominent clients.

AVOID THESE MICRO-NICHE BUILDING MISTAKES:

1. Too many CPAs look at their client list, find four or five people to whom they provide similar service, and fail to start advertising their service to that micro-niche.
2. Too many CPA firms try to build micro-niches without help from experts. How would entrepreneurs succeed in doing tax planning?
3. Too many firms fail to create and follow a carefully designed process in all efforts and communication with the micro-niche.
4. Too many firms build a micro-niche and fail to develop it into a boutique business because they fail to provide a unique customer experience for boutique clients.

Depending upon the amount of change in the area of your expertise, hold a quarterly, semi-annual or annual seminar for your micro-niche clients. Use the event as a way to demonstrate appreciation for the client and an opportunity for the client to learn new information that will make him or her more successful.

These ideas can begin your thinking about ways you wish to make your clients feel they are receiving a higher-quality customer experience when they do business with your micro-niche boutique. It helps to remember that even accounting clients are people. Their shopping and buying experiences with other companies set the bar (consciously or unconsciously) for their client service expectations, especially when they are paying premium prices for your services and expertise. So when you look at your level of service do not compare it to your competitor but to the best.

7

The Right People
for Your Micro-Niche
Boutique

• 7 •

The Right People for Your Micro-Niche Boutique

Building a successful and profitable micro-niche boutique in your firm depends upon your ability to build a business around the expertise of a partner or member of the firm. The market might be telling you what your firm does particularly well. You might quickly identify the experts in these high-demand areas. You might also discover that one or more of your staff would like to cultivate expertise and build a boutique business in an area that would draw in new highly profitable clients. To which partners or staff should you look for the leadership and expertise that can be the basis for a micro-niche boutique?

Who are the right people in your firm to be your experts or the leaders of the micro-niche boutiques you will build? The four main categories of potential micro-niche experts are:

1. **Partners looking to re-energize a successful book**

   Many firms can use development of a micro-niche boutique to re-energize a successful book. Typically, any successful book will include some predominance of a particular type of work. This might be a specific service provided to a particular class of clients. It might be a group of services provided to clients in a particular industry. Adding a micro-niche specialty related to the currently successful book can often energize both the book and the individual.

2. **Technical partners**

Technical partners are those who have valuable skills in an area related to the firm's business that could become a new product or service needed by a number of the firm's clients. Unfortunately, these partners typically cannot bring in business, so they really are not maximizing their upside either personally or for the firm. A micro-niche boutique will allow them not only to bring in business, but to bring in the premium business that their technical skills should allow them to. Although these people often have been written off in terms of their ability to bring in new business, the micro-niche focus makes them feel unique in the marketplace and gives them the confidence to actually do the activities that will bring in business.

3. **New partners/directors/principals**

New partners, directors and/or principals bring to the firm opportunity to capitalize on their previous experience and expertise. They might bring with them a developing book containing the foundation of a niche business. New partners, as their book indicates, have probably demonstrated some rainmaking ability. If they have begun to develop a specialty, a micro-niche boutique offers the opportunity to develop further both rainmaking skill and expertise in a micro-niche area. Paired with a strong technical person with the management and customer service skills needed, a strong boutique business could emerge.

4. **A partner of the future**

Because micro-niche boutique development requires a relatively small investment by the firm, the opportunity to build and grow a boutique can be an opportunity for a partner of the future to prove him- or herself and earn partner status. This option provides relative autonomy (as much as the firm is comfortable allowing), unlimited opportunity and a unique incentive program for a promising young staffer. Growing a micro-niche and building a boutique can be an excellent way to cultivate confidence and stature in young staffers or partners and allow them to "own" their expertise.

Each of the people listed offers a unique opportunity to expand the services offered by your firm, as well as creating a practice area that will draw new clients and sell additional services to both new and current clients. As you should have learned from the process of creating and marketing practice niches, your micro-niche boutique will breathe new life into the firm and create new opportunities to grow your business strategically.

Drawing upon partners or other staff members in one of these four categories should allow your firm to make a strong beginning building a micro-niche boutique within the business. You might select someone for a micro-niche who wants to revitalize his or her career, someone within the firm who has needed and marketable technical skills or someone for who you want to provide opportunity to grow. Regardless of your motive in selecting the expert around whom you will build the micro-niche, a well-chosen micro-niche built into a boutique business will increase top-line revenue, profitability and the reputation of the firm.

8

Marketing

• 8 •

Marketing

They say that if you build a better mousetrap, the world will beat a path to your door. Don't count on it. You need to be proactive. If you effectively *market* your new mousetrap, you will reap bigger rewards and you will reap them more quickly than your competitors.

To position your boutique service within the competitive marketplace, you need an effective marketing approach that integrates a number of strategies. Each strategy will be selected because it is calculated to contribute to an overall marketing goal. An **integrated strategy** is designed in order to have each strategy reinforce another strategy effectively.

You will want to select the marketing strategies that enable you to tell your ideal clients about how you can help them. You need to keep the focus always on what is important to your ideal clients and not on yourself.

You need to choose the marketing strategies that you are comfortable using and that are most appropriate and effective for your ideal client. For example, if you are marketing a CPA firm that caters exclusively to large global corporations, Facebook (no matter how popular) is probably not the best match of message and medium. Or if you have a tremendous fear of public speaking, this should not be part of your strategy.

Message and Budget

Once you define and describe your ideal client you will know how to address that client. You can then refine your messaging. Keep every message directed to the ideal client in tone, vocabulary, and style. Then you will choose, prioritize and schedule each marketing strategy you believe appropriate to convince your ideal client that you have the expertise to solve his problems or meet her needs.

Next, you will need to establish a budget for your marketing plan.

You will then be ready to evaluate the appropriateness of the various marketing strategies available to you. The boundaries of your micro-niche, your message and your budget will establish limits for your marketing strategy and plan.

Your Power Phrase

What is a power phrase? It's any phrase that you use naturally through the course of your day when you talk with clients, which seems to resonate and make the listener more excited. When you use these terms people respond in a positive way and they understand that you have something special to offer.

For example, a CPA who focuses on due diligence often says, "I help make deals happen." Why is this a power phrase? Because many clients have the perception that most CPAs *kill* deals. Saying "I make deals happen" serves to overcome a common objection and put the client at ease.

Another power phrase from the same CPA was, "When we find something as part of our due diligence we will discuss how to make it into the best negotiating chip we can." Once again, you are transforming a negative into a positive.

What usually happens is that during the normal course of a conversation, opportunities present themselves to use them. The best way to choose a power phrase is to have conversations with clients and COIs and see what resonates with them. It comes from talking and listening.

Marketing Materials

Despite the revolutionary changes introduced by new technologies, most firms find they still need to straddle the divide, keeping one foot in traditional marketing and the other in Internet marketing. Fortunately (at least for the budget) the need to remain consistent in graphic imagery, content, style and message will often allow you to create marketing collateral in both traditional and digital format at the same time with only modest changes.

For example, your company brochure and marketing kit will take two forms: (1) printed on high quality paper and placed in an attractive folder and (2) as the basis for your website. Another alternative, however, is to produce only a digital form of the marketing kit, use it as the basis for your website, and use it as your traditional marketing kit by copying it to a disc that resembles and is printed to copy a business card, or copy it to an inexpensive flash drive.

LEVERAGE YOUR EXPERTISE WITH TARGETED MARKETING

With a micro-niche boutique, marketing your CPA firm becomes more efficient. Instead of a scattershot approach where you're never sure whom your message is reaching, your marketing is targeted directly at the clients you want. Your marketing budget and your networking time will go much further and produce measurable results.

Remember, marketing materials are important to back up what you say. Especially in the beginning, effective marketing will be you, networking, speaking, and writing. No one buys a brochure – people still buy people.

Your marketing approach will combine marketing and public relations activities and will inevitably draw upon some of the following:

Internet and media

- Website

- Webinars

- Article marketing/Content publication

- Distribution of free reports for list building

- Media campaigns

- Internet advertising

- Blogging

- Local search optimization

- Authority building

- Social networking

Traditional print

- Press kit

- Marketing kit

- Strategic plan

- Publication of white papers and e-books

- Business plan

- Company brochure

- Micro-niche business brochure

- Traditional advertising

Personal

- Building strong industry relationships

- Speaking campaign

- Networking, particularly within your micro-niche industry

- Sales campaigns

Building strong industry relationships is probably the most important key to building your business by building a micro-niche. You will experience some success with advertising. You will certainly have some growth success through client referrals.

Conduct appropriate keyword research for your micro-niche and ensure that your website is search engine optimized and designed to appeal to your ideal clients and the terms they are likely to use to find the services and products you offer.

Refer back to the analysis you did in defining your niche to the description of your ideal client. This insight is critical in planning your marketing strategy when you start building a micro-niche. The client profile will help you keep your messages focused on the most important audience and it will help you clarify your value proposition. You will know what benefits of your services are most important to this ideal client. You will understand what problems the ideal client faces and you will be able to explain how you can satisfy the client's basic needs.

If your ideal client is a business, you need to establish some criteria by which you qualify the business as a client, and find the intersection of their needs and your expertise. These qualifications might include annual sales volume, number of employees, location, industry, type of specific CPA service needs, company history, purchasing practices, or corporate policies. It is important to invest the time to do the research so you understand any company you hope to do business with.

Building recognition of your expertise in your micro-niche is at least half of the goal of all of your marketing efforts. Your ideal clients will seek you out and do business with you because they perceive you as an expert. When you are perceived as an expert in your micro-niche, a number of other opportunities also become open to you, such as:

- Speaking
- Writing and publishing expert books
- Consulting

Many of the critical skills and abilities necessary for practice building are not part of the core competencies of most CPAs. There is no negative implication in this statement. It is also probable that members of your staff do not have a great deal of time to invest in practice development, even those who will be key players in the new micro-niche boutique.

There are several ways to strengthen your marketing skills.

First, you can outsource each of the tasks and skill-sets you think you need to accomplish your goals.

Second, you can invest the time and the money in training your staff to accomplish each of the tasks and goals.

Third, you can engage a consulting firm, like The Practice Building Team, to provide the skills and knowledge you need, to produce the work that is not among your staff's core competencies, and train and mentor your staff in the skills they will need. This kind of team will provide or engage the experts in business development, firm management, market research, marketing, Internet marketing, web development, content planning and production, and training and mentoring of your staff.

9

Show Me
the Money

• 9 •

Show Me the Money

Every business needs financial planning. Your CPA firm is no different. A key component to selecting and building a micro-niche boutique is making a sensible projection of the impact it will have on your partnership or firm. If, after doing the math, the numbers just don't make it feasible, then don't do it. But chances are, if you put together a micro-niche that includes your expertise and a need expressed by one or more clients, you will see that the financial rewards will be significant.

Every firm's comp program is different. Some are open and transparent and some are the black box of comp committee rules. One thing is consistent – people who are the rainmakers in the firm are the high earners. So adding or starting your book of business will almost always increase the individual's pay.

Almost all CPA firms are run efficiently. It is difficult to add significantly to the bottom line by being even more efficient. For most firms the path to an increased bottom line is to *grow* – and the Micro-niche method™ is designed to help your firm grow.

Look at your own firm. Do your own math. Think about what an increase to the top line with high realization and premium pricing will do to the bottom line. Can you afford not to explore making this happen in your firm?

10

The Importance of Networking

• 10 •

The Importance of Networking

The way your firm will experience the kind of growth you want will be through the relationships you build within the industry and with key COIs. So, how do you make that happen?

In building industry relationships and creating the messaging you will use in your marketing campaigns, you must walk a very fine line between boasting and explaining, and between over-promising and under-valuing your expertise. With that being said I have found that although many accountants will feel they are close to that line the vast majority never approach it – it just is not who you are. You must find the right way to tell the industry you understand it and the needs of companies within the industry.

As you build these relationships, you increase your visibility as an industry insider and expert. In short, the best way to build your visibility and your share of the market you want to dominate is to build relationships that will open doors. This fact makes professional networking one of your most important marketing activities.

You build the relationships that can grow your business by becoming involved in as many aspects of the industry as possible:

- Attend meetings, conferences and trade shows.

- Write about your knowledge of the industry and how your knowledge helps your clients achieve their business goals.

- Make yourself and your knowledge available as a speaker at events and gatherings.

- Talk to everyone you can to make your name a "household word" throughout the industry.

- Get to know and be known by leading journalists covering the industry and other industry experts.

- Offer positive, helpful and thoughtful responses to product reviews, magazine and newspaper articles, blogs and other industry news and insights, join social media groups relevant to the industry.

- Volunteer for committees.

Depth, Not Breadth

During the course of your career, someone has probably told you to write and practice an "elevator pitch." In fact, there are people who have written books about elevator speeches. They encourage you to work hard on writing, rehearsing and refining your elevator pitch.

I do not think this is a worthwhile use of your time. I cannot speak for anyone else, but I have never been in an elevator where somebody shared an elevator speech. I also have never been in an elevator when I had taken the opportunity to make an "elevator pitch."

A number of business coaches will tell you to attend networking events and use your elevator pitch to make valuable contacts, get referrals and win customers. I have done that. I have attended networking events and made my pitch to a room full of people. The bottom line is that it never paid off in a significant way. If you are in the business of collecting business cards, these events are probably worthwhile.

My experience with big networking events, where everyone stands up and has thirty seconds to say who they are, has been that the people who spoke before me were settling into their seats and relaxing while I was making my presentation. The people who were to speak after me were getting ready to make their presentation. Nobody was really paying attention. Thus, for my money, these big networking events are not effective. They are not a good use of time.

Instead, you need to focus your efforts on the right people. You need depth, not just breadth.

You must choose the right places to go to meet the right people. As I indicated earlier, I do not think the right place is likely to be a huge networking meeting. Instead, I suggest asking business associates for introductions to people who might be a good source of referrals. You will want to get to know other CPAs – and become known by them for your micro-niche. Various gatherings of CPAs will be a good starting point (AICPA, your state group, etc.). You should also become very active in other groups as well: industry organizations, the local bar association, local bankers and those attended by other influencers and referral sources. You can work through local associations of business owners, such as the chamber of commerce. Do not overlook organizations like the National Association of Woman-Owned Businesses, similar associations of minority business owners or veterans' business owners.

How to Answer the Question,
"What Do You Do?"

When you meet someone, a common question is, "What do you do?" When I teach networking, about ninety percent of the people in the group or seminar say they tell people, "I'm an accountant." A few others will tell people they are a CPA or a partner in an accounting firm.

These are the standard replies. The standard result is that the conversation moves to another topic or simply dies because people think there is nothing to say or, like many who are not accountants, they think the subject of accounting is boring.

They are not being mean; it's just that for most people the mechanics of accounting are, well, boring. All those columns of numbers! What isn't boring are the results of accounting. When you tell your client that you just saved them ten thousand dollars on their taxes, that's exciting! You've just helped them buy a new car or a trip to Europe.

You need to tell people that what you do is help your clients save money. Big money.

Here is an example. I have a friend who has a high-tech local search company. He is starting to think about taking the company public. I told him I work with many accountants. He responded, "Oh. We are good with our accountant." The conversation switched to another topic quickly.

But I persisted and said, "I work with an accountant who specializes in helping tech companies go public. He has done that with six clients, taking them through the whole process, getting SEC approval and all the other steps. Then he helps them raise the money." Then I asked, "Would you like to be introduced to this accountant?"

This time, he said, "Set up a lunch."

My friend's response went from, "We like our accountant" to "This person might bring something to the table that we need." This is why it is so important to have a good answer to the question of what you do.

This is not an elevator speech. It is not a pre-written, planned and rehearsed sales or marketing pitch. It will vary depending on whom you're talking to. It is the answer to a question about what you do, but it immediately creates a connection with the other person by identifying a way you can help him/her.

YOUR POWER PHRASE

Not everyone is a "born salesperson." With the Micro-Niche Method™, you don't have to be. All you need to do is tell prospective clients how you can *benefit* them. After all, that's all they really care about! With a succinct power phrase, you can let the client know that you have the solution to their pain. If they ask "How?" then you know you're halfway to having a new client.

Think about the level of interest you will create in a banker with each of these responses to the question, "What do you do?"

1. "I'm an accountant." Boring.

2. "I'm a partner in an accounting firm." Still boring.

3. "I help growing companies identify and take advantage of any tax credits for adding employees or adding space." Now that's interesting! The accountant part can come at the end of this or thirty seconds later in the conversation.

This should help you understand the difference between repeating a pre-written speech at some big networking event that is more devoted to building the size of your contact list than helping you actually build your practice and answering a simple question in a way that immediately explains your expertise and creates a connection with another person.

Now, it is time to think about where you should try to meet and engage people who can help you build your practice.

Centers of Influence

Instead of wasting time attending networking events unlikely to produce the kind of results you need, focus on centers of influence. I define "center of influence" as someone – often another accounting firm, a banker, or attorney – who can send clients/business to you on a regular basis.

The real value of centers of influence is that they can deliver prospects to you who are looking for your specific expertise and are ready to buy from you, and they can do it on a consistent basis.

The prospects delivered by centers of influence are pre-qualified prospects ready to buy. They are not putting out a RFP in which you must compete. They are not interviewing other accountants against whom they will evaluate you. They will confirm that you can do what they need, and then engage you.

When I outlined the differences between being a commodity and being an expert, I mentioned referrals. The kind of referrals you receive will indicate that you have become an expert because your Centers of Influence will stop looking at you as a quid-pro-quo referral source. They will no longer send opportunities to you with the expectation that you will reciprocate. You do not want to be in that situation with a center of influence because you can only reciprocate with a few referrals. Centers of Influence take you out of commodity relationships. In the new scenario, they will look at you and give you referrals because you can truly solve the client's problem.

When you approach centers of influence, you must remember that you are not offering an elevator pitch. You will never tell a center of influence that you are an accountant in your first sentence. They already know many accountants and being just another accountant will not command their attention. Instead, you will be thinking about what is important to them and to their clients. If you build your micro-niche properly, there are not a million alternatives – there is only you.

If you try to market or sell your expertise in an undifferentiated marketplace (like a networking session), it is like going to a cattle call. It is very hard to identify clients with the right need at the right time. If, on the other hand, you have centers of influence, and you maintain those relationships effectively, you can count on the center of influence to make the connection and send the client to you when the need arises.

You can go to a thousand networking events and get one client every now and then. If you have ten centers of influence and each gives you two or three high-quality clients per year, you can build a big book of business.

Conclusion

Conclusion

If you are serious about building your practice, you will find that building a micro-niche boutique is strong business strategy with a high rate of success. People trust experts. Our society shows a clear preference for doing business with people we know, trust and respect. Establishing and promoting your expertise as the focus of your business activities will enable you to charge premium rates and transform your business from a commodity to a sought-after resource.

You already know that in the business world, few things that have the power to happen overnight. You also know that if you want your business to succeed you must invest the time and effort necessary to make it succeed. Building a business that responds to the needs of a specific set of potential clients is no different.

If you can keep your eye on the goal and make carefully considered choices based on solid research, you can define a micro-niche and build a thriving business around it. Only you can decide what that micro-niche will be. You must then make good choices about the marketing strategies you will use to deliver the right message in the right words in the right medium to the right audience at the right time.

If you are willing to do the work and invest the effort, you can build a successful micro-niche business that will significantly grow your practice. Take the time you need in making decisions. Do the research, learn what you need to learn, and market wisely. Finally, make sure you enjoy the kind of work you will be doing with the kind of people who will become your clients.

About the
Practice Building Team

About The Practice Building Team

Many accounting and CPA firms are discovering a new environment in which they must market their services and differentiate their practices from competing firms. At the same time, many CPAs are realizing that the state of the profession has relegated them to commodity status.

The Practice Building Team helps accounting firms discover the means of achieving the kind of growth and increased profitability they need to remain competitive and viable. The consultancy focuses of the following key growth strategies:

- Increasing wallet share from current clients by creating new accounting service offerings and selling new and existing accounting services to current clients; addition of new advisory services, such as financial planning or wealth management

- Building micro-niche businesses based on the current strengths and expertise of partners

- Future partners programs

Each of these key strategies begins with existing staff and skills or adds services through partnerships with or acquisition of another firm. The first two strategies increase profitability by selling additional services to current clients. Micro-Niche development as a growth strategy, the unique approach created by President and CEO David

Wolfskehl, begins with the particular skills and interests of the partner or associate of the firm. Once a specific area of expertise is delineated attention focuses on cultivating the expertise of the CPA and marketing the premium-priced micro-niche services. With this three-pronged approach, CPA firms are discovering greater profitability and significant practice growth.

In addition to these efforts, and for those who joined the profession more recently, The Practice Building Team offers Future Partner Programs. These programs work with future partners, teaching them the soft skills and business development skills needed to maximize their strengths and knowledge, and helping them build the confidence to work toward a fulfilling partnership.

About
David Wolfskehl

About David Wolfskehl

David Wolfskehl is a lifelong entrepreneur and a guide for entrepreneurs. He is a widely respected author and speaker. As President and CEO of The Practice Building Team, David helps CPAs increase wallet share from current clients by selling them additional services offered by the firm, grow their firms by adding new advisory services (such as wealth management), maximize opportunities if they currently provide advisory services and define and build powerful micro-niche businesses that redefine success and professional excellence. Because micro-niches are built upon the expertise of a single accountant, they stand alone in the marketplace and justify premium pricing for services. The Practice Building Team's Future Partner Programs teach future CPA firm partners how to build a book of business.

After graduation from the University of Arizona, David started A Bridgewater Copy and Print. Remaining within the printing industry for the next 17 years, David next started In A Bind, and later merged his operation with Action Fast Print. Action Fast Print became the second largest quick printer in New Jersey for 2002-2004, according to NJBIZ. David is married and has two children.

David is the author of *The Micro-Niche Method: The Pathway to Premium Pricing and Increased Profitability for Today's CPAs*. To learn more, or to purchase a copy of the book, please visit Amazon.com, your local bookseller or http://www.themicronichemethod.com. The book is a step-by-step guide for accountants who wish to identify, evaluate and build a micro-niche business. It includes sections on assessment of potential micro-niches, implementation of the operational and marketing needs of the micro-niche business, and how to scale back marketing efforts to maintain your "go-to" status.

David believes passionately in the importance of entrepreneurs interacting. To facilitate such interaction, he fulfills the following roles:

- Three-year board member of the Entrepreneur Organization

- Executive committee board member for the Somerset County Business Partnership

- Entrepreneur in Residence and Vice-Chair of IFEL, an idea incubator located on the NJIT campus, which not only helps budding entrepreneurs, but also works in economic development in urban areas.

David has received several business awards, including:

- ARC employer of the year

- Fortune Small Business Magazine Boss of the Year finalist

Learn more about David and about The Practice Building Team at http://www.tpbteam.com. Read our micro-niche building blog at http://themicronichemethod.com.

For speaking or consulting engagements please call

908 393 2722

david@tpbteam.com

Made in the USA
Charleston, SC
26 October 2011